Farfetched: What Foreign Poems

For Gill and Elaine

Wherever possible I have reproduced relevant poems, extracts and translations into English. Where I do not have the right to do so, I have included details of websites where they can be found.

I am grateful to the following for suggesting poems and generously giving their time to help me to understand them:

Celine Caquineau, Wilson McLeod, Felipe Sanchez Burgos, Konstantina Zerva, Smaragda Tsairidou, Sofia Shan, Nancy Mutshaeni, Thomas Bak, Mourad Diouri, Maria Grade Godinho, Gaia del Negro.

Introduction

A writer only begins a book. A reader finishes it.

There's much to be said for this statement, attributed to Samuel Johnson, although I wonder if a book is ever really finished. Poetry in particular 'leaves frayed edges and loose wires' (McBride). I have begun this book for you but I've left lots of loose ends so that you can make your own connections. I've also left plenty of white space for you to fill with anything you wish. I hope you enjoy it.

Farfetched

This book tells stories of my encounters with 11 foreign language poems and how I tried to make sense of them, with a little help from my friends. In the spring of 2020, I had just retired from the University of Edinburgh and was immediately sent into lockdown by the Coronavirus. I had time to read and write, and the chance to think while I trundled my tricycle along the quiet lanes near my home. I became aware that I had contact with a number of intriguing people, who spoke a range of enticing languages. I decided I would invite some of them to choose a short poem in their first language and ask them to help me to make sense of it. I set myself the challenge of 10 poems in 10 languages. In the end it turned out to be 11 poems, because Greek insisted on appearing twice.

So why the title: Far-fetched? Originally referring to an item brought from a long way away, and for that reason desirable and interesting, it eventually came to mean something unlikely and implausible. It was just when exotic commodities were being introduced in Elizabethan England that "far-fetched" began to shift its meaning. In his classic 1963 skit, the US comedian Bob Newhart imagines Sir Walter ('Nutty Walt') Raleigh telephoning from the Colonies about the commercial potential of newly-discovered 'toe-back-oh.' The head of the trading company back in England is unimpressed when the hapless Walt tries to explain the potential of tobacco:

"you can shred it up…and put it on a piece of paper…and roll it up….Don't tell me Walt, don't tell me. ..You stick it in your ear right? …Oh! between your lips!...Then what do you do Walt? You set fire to it! Then what do you do, Walt? You inhale the smoke!"

This book is far-fetched in the earlier sense – I am bringing you poems from far away, in both geography and time. They have the allure of the unfamiliar. I am aware that I also come close to that farfetchedness that is weird, ridiculous and stretches credibility. Is there really any point in trying to read a poem in a language you do not understand? I am convinced that there is, but you can judge for yourself.

What do you think?

Chapter 1 In which we meet the Author before she could read or write. The Art of Close Reading is introduced. The Author recommends the reading of poems in foreign Languages and explains the Origins of this Book.

She can read anything

I'm watching a police drama on the telly in the 1960s: Dixon of Dock Green, or possibly Z-cars. A man is released from prison on his daughter's wedding day, and is desperately trying to get to the church in time to see her married. On the way he stops to buy some children's comics as a wedding present. It's clear that the man can't read, and the shopkeeper asks if he's sure that they are what his daughter would want. "Oh yes," he says proudly, "She can read anything."

This exchange has stayed with me for more than 50 years. At the time I just found it sad, but later I became aware of the pain of a child knowing more than a parent. I also noticed the strange assumption that people who can't read, know nothing about reading. Of course the old man would know that comics are for children, even though he hadn't learned to read himself. In my experience people who are excluded from the literate world tend to be very well-informed about what they are missing.

Certainly I knew about reading and its importance long before I could do it myself. I begged Mum to teach me letters, so she gave me a pencil and paper and one of her handkerchiefs, embroidered with a capital E (for Eunice) for me to copy. I managed the down stroke, no problem, but when it came to the horizontal lines it ended up looking like a scrubbing brush. Mum said it was wrong, I had done too many lines, but I didn't understand. How many was enough?

I have never been a voracious reader. The idea of devouring vast quantities of books at speed does not appeal to me. Nor do I escape through poetry into an alternative reality. Reading has always seemed to me to be an experience very much of this world, like a walk in the wind, a bowl of soup or the trying on of a nice new pair of socks. I like short poems, handfuls of language that I can carry about with me and I really like thinking about individual words.

Close reading

As a child I used to spend hours knitting, struggling with yarn and needles, tongue poked out in concentration, chanting "in, round, through, off, in, round, through off" but I don't remember ever completing a wearable garment. If anything sexy came on the telly, Mum shouted "Get on with your knitting!" and I'd stare hard at my wobbly stitches, until the embarrassment passed. Luckily, this led to only a mild wool fetish later in life. But I think it did reinforce my tendency to focus on details and blot out the bigger picture. When I'm reading I always like to zoom in on a single word and to let the wider context fall away.

I was an undergraduate in the 1970s, studying the ambitiously-titled English Literature, Life and Thought (it was a three-year course) when I was introduced to the art of Practical Criticism. Every week we were presented with a short piece of poetry, undated and anonymous, and asked to come up with an 'authentic response.' I loved Practical Criticism. My fellow students seemed to be very well-read and were confident with both primary and secondary texts. I didn't know my Auden from my Eliot, but I enjoyed coming face to face with a poem and exploring it, looking for patterns, feeling textures, making connections and conjectures. It was such a relief that I didn't have to know what other people had said about a poem before I could make my own comments. In particular I loved examining individual words. When it came to exam time, there were often scary rumours that we would be given a page of a telephone directory to analyse. I honestly think I could have done that. I've had many an insight from a sauce bottle or cereal packet, usually during the course of an awkward breakfast.

One of our Practical Criticism tutors introduced us to a short poem (I can't remember which) and suggested we examine the prepositions and adverbs. It was a good lesson in paying attention to what is often overlooked. The following week, working on another piece, we all, unsurprisingly, found deep meaning in the prepositions and adverbs. That time the lesson was how we sometimes miss the point.

I very nearly ended up spending my life reading very closely indeed. In 1979 I worked as a research assistant on a project led by Professor Clemoes in the Department of Anglo-Saxon, Norse and Celtic at the University of Cambridge. Beowulf is the hero of an ancient poem who kills a horrible monster called Grendel. Grendel's mother turns out to be even more horrible and so he kills her as well. (There is, of course, more to it than that). Professor Clemoes told me that, rather disturbingly, he was passionately interested in dating Beowulf. I readily agreed to help when I understood that he wanted to establish in what year the poem was written. He had a theory that this could be determined, at least in part, by paying attention to stylistic traits, and in particular to the occurrence of pairs of words connected with "and" : kith and kin, born and bred, hell and high water. In order to make his argument, he needed to compare the frequency of this construction in Beowulf with other Anglo-Saxon writings, so he paid me to count them.

I made a good start, confident that this was my way in to the glorious world of literary research. The spirit was willing, but the body was oh so much more sensible. I developed, for the first and last time in my life a nasty condition that starts with an infernal itch in your eye and then a thick unpleasant discharge that glues it firmly shut. If you're really unlucky (I was) when you lie down to sleep, some of the gunk drips from the infected eye into the clean eye, sealing up both of them and making it difficult to read, and practically impossible to count all the pairs of words connected with "and" in the entire Anglo-Saxon poetic corpus.

I knew my body was wise, but I didn't realise until very recently that it is witty as well. The condition that stopped me from devoting my life to that rather tedious twiglet of literary research was…conjunctivitis.

What does 'close reading' mean to you?

Reading poems in foreign languages

I recommend reading foreign poems for the same reason that I recommend foreign travel: to see different sights and to hear different sounds, to smell different smells and to feel different weather on your skin, to be abroad. Now there's a lovely word: abroad. It suggests to me being at large, free, away from the narrowness of home.

If you Google "abroad means" you get a list of definitions, derivations and examples of usage and then in one of my favourite places on the internet, the "People also ask…" section, a poignant set of questions:

Which country is called as abroad?

What is an example of abroad?

What means going abroad?

Is Canada considered abroad?

In all their earnestness and wonky grammar, the questions 'people also ask' seem to be important. In response to the last query, someone has written:

Why or why not? Yes, flying from the United States to Canada or from Canada to the United States is considered to be international travel. I note the broad promise of the initial question and then the assumption that we are all in North America.

My estranged sister enjoyed travelling and would declare, quite without irony, that wherever she went in the world she was never a foreigner because she was always English. I also love travelling, but for me being foreign is a good thing: a comfortable, explicable way of being different from the people around me. In my twenties I worked abroad Teaching English as a Foreign Language. I like that phrase with its reminder that it's possible to see something familiar from a different perspective – the "as" that invariably escaped my sister.

I have always had a terrible sense of direction. People who knew me as a child were surprised when I grew up to be an independent traveller. What they didn't realise was, that if you've never had your bearings, you can't lose them. It was no more unsettling for me to get lost in Lisbon or Cairo than to be disorientated in the tiny village where I grew up. So it is with poetry. Any poem is a foreign country, and a foreign poem is not necessarily more inaccessible than one in your own language.

Of course I can't do it all by myself. Translations are a great help, even though they can never replace the original. Parallel texts are fun: I love jumping between them, trying to catch sight of something. And native speakers are a great resource. I feel lucky to have friends and colleagues who are willing to spend time helping me and answering my daft questions. In fact, those questions are well worth asking, because sometimes an outsider can notice things that a reader familiar with the language might miss.

If by any chance one of the poems in this book is in your first language, then you are lucky. You will enjoy an intimacy with the poem, each of its words and all its associations that the rest of us can only imagine. If you don't know a single word of these languages then you are also lucky. You'll be able to hear the sounds or see the shapes of the poems directly, freshly, without anything getting in the way. Perhaps you find yourself in between these two extremes. You may have studied the language at school, travelled abroad, used a phrase book or recognise a few common words. In that case, you are really lucky, because you will have your own unique combination of knowing and not knowing, understanding and misunderstanding.

What do you miss when you read or hear a poem in an unfamiliar language?

What do you notice?

Well, do you think it's possible to make sense of poems in unfamiliar languages?

Chapter 2, in which the Author encounters a foreign Language for the first Time. She gains Insight from a Mistranslation and comes across Enantiosemy.

Et un Sourire by Paul Eluard can be found here:
http://www.unjourunpoeme.fr/poeme/et-un-sourire

It is never completely night.

There is always, since I say so,

Since I assert it,

At the end of the grief

An open window

A lighted window.

There is always a dream that keeps watch,

A desire to be fulfilled,

Hunger to satisfy,

A generous heart,

a hand held out,

an open hand,

attentive eyes

a life: the life to be shared.

English translation: Daphne Loads

Such magical possibilities

By the time I was four, my two older sisters were already learning French at school. Neither seemed very enthusiastic about the experience, but I always pestered them to repeat those fascinating sounds and to tell me what they meant. This was my first encounter with anything foreign and it made a big impression on me. Once when I found a ladybird-like creature in the garden with a different pattern from the usual red and black spots, I ran in excitedly: "Look, it's French! It's a French ladybird!"

At Primary School, Linda Lamington confidently explained that a French word always rhymes with its English equivalent. She also told me about boys' willies. It turned out Linda was better at anatomy than languages.

When we began to study French for real, it came easily to me. At fourteen, I went to Orleans on a school trip and gained a confidence I had never known before. Painfully shy and tongue-tied in English, I found that in French the words just unfolded from my mouth. And at university, I discovered French poetry. I can distinctly remember reading Verlaine one wet rail journey to Cambridge. Many years later, when I heard the song Girl on the Train by Clive James and Pete Atkin I thought, "That could have been me."

"But she kept on the job of improving her single-track brain

Ploughing steadily onward through obsolete Monsieur Verlaine

While no further than seven-foot-six from her fabulous mouth

Sat the leading young poetic hope of the whole planet earth…"

Clive James used to live in Cambridge and, despite the fact that I remember my student self as dismally podgy and pale, there's just a chance that in a lonely moment one rainy afternoon, he might have described my mouth as fabulous. French has always had such magical possibilities.

All the ambiguities

Sometimes a poem can accommodate idiosyncratic interpretations. The misguided, the wildly improbable, even the simply wrong can become a part of its fabric, just as ivy becomes a part of the structure of an old house. (See my mother's reading of Ode to Spring in Chapter 7 and Christopher Pine's penis in Chapter 2). At first it seemed that the French poem that Celine had chosen for me was not such a piece. In "Et un sourire" by Paul Eluard, there seemed to be no place for ivy on its smooth surface. Celine was surprised, even a little embarrassed by her own choice. It wasn't the kind of poem she would turn to ordinarily. But these were not ordinary times: Coronavirus had struck, and lockdown had just started. She remembered the last time this poem had meant something to her, during the Charlie Hebdaire crisis.

I shared her unease. This was a poem that seemed a little too comfortable to be truly comforting. Because I had read that Eluard was a Dadaist, I was on the lookout for irony or playfulness, for contradictions that might undercut the smooth surface of his reassurances. I found none, until Celine drew attention to "puisque je le dis," "since I say so." This, her favourite part of the poem, "creates all the ambiguities," she said. "Is he confident? Or does he need to reassure himself? Or is he trying to convince us as well?" I think she may be on to something there.

Mistaking

On the internet I found a version of Eluard's poem poignantly mistranslated from French to English that had been offered, apparently in good faith, by a speaker of a third language. The "main tendue" that I understood as "an outstretched hand" was translated as "a tense hand" and the final line that for me was "the life to be shared" had become "the life to be divided." So in even the plainest of poems, there is always the potential for welcome to become tension and for sharing to give way to division.

It reminds me of a lecture I once attended that was given by Christopher Ricks. In those days before the rise of the celebrity academic, he was rather a trendy figure, partly because he spoke of the lyrics of Bob Dylan in the same breath as the poetry of Milton and Keats. Ricks was talking about word origins and the way that, if you go back far enough in their etymologies, words often move close to their opposites. He gave the example of 'host' and 'hostile.' I felt the thrilling sensation of certainties cracking beneath my feet. I loved the idea that words could be so fascinating and so unreliable. It seemed to suggest to me a universe full of possibilities. Since then I have always had a liking for ambiguity and contradiction in poetry from Shakespeare to Emily Dickinson. In fact, in the interviews for this book, I explicitly asked participants "What ambiguities and contradictions are you aware of?" Anatoly Lieberman dismisses romanticisation of this phenomemon in his discussion of enantiosemy –

"It means a combination of two opposite senses in one word, as in Latin altus "high" and "deep." Some people have spun an intricate yarn around this phenomenon, pointing out that everything in the world has two sides … Etymology shows that the distance from host to guest, from friend to enemy, and from love to hatred is short, but we do not need historical linguists to tell us that."

I wonder if the clumsy translator of Eluard's poem had any inkling of his errors: for me, knowing that someone is unknowingly mistaken is sometimes unbearably poignant. I think this dates back to my childhood when I began to suspect that my mother knew even less about the world than I did.

Mistaking

Mum used to bake Victoria sponges that didn't rise: they always turned out heavy and sad. Frustrated, she would re-read the recipe in her Be-Ro book. "Foundation recipe: Two eggs, 4oz sugar, 4oz Be-Ro self-raising flour." She came up with an explanation: it was a 'foundation' recipe, and that was why her cakes turned out so solid.

I absorbed her frustration, the sadness of the flat cakes, the repeated disappointments. I knew that foundation just meant basic, as opposed to the variations of chocolate or strawberry and I felt a kind of wretched regret that I understood this and she didn't. I knew that she was wrong about other things too: that divers places in the Bible weren't necessarily under the sea, that quotations from 'Pope' in the Readers' Digest had not been spoken by His Holiness. There were other things I suspected she was wrong about – like it being better to save up my wee and go at home, rather than risk catching something in the school toilets; that a sewing needle lost in a bed could get into your veins and kill you. Very occasionally I would challenge her, but I always seemed to choose the wrong battles. Once I tried to convince her to ask the newsagent for her weekly "Reveille" with a French 'r' and pouted lips, because "riVALLey" was just plain wrong. By the way, I recently googled Reveille. I'd always assumed from its faux military title that it was one of her Salvation Army papers, but no, it was a rather racy publication stuffed with scandal. That time it was I who was wrong.

What mistakes have you made in reading poetry? Did anything good come of them?

Chapter 3 in which the Author is introduced to Scottish Gaelic, participates in an ill-advised Research Project and after Some Time experiences a Superb Surprise. She goes in search of Mysterious Birds and Christopher Pine's Penis pops up.

Hallaig by Sorely MacLean can be found here:
https://www.scottishpoetrylibrary.org.uk/poem/hallaig/

Imagine you are in a lift

I am at an event at the Edinburgh Book Festival, and a poet is reading his poems. At first he reads in Gaelic. Then he reads his own English translation of his own poem. But between the two readings, everything changes. His posture, his gestures, his movement, the feeling in the room. What is happening?

I had long been drawn to the idea of Gaelic, but I first started studying the language three years ago with a delightfully mad young woman who gave evening classes at the university where I worked. She taught us the meaning of the word 'air' (on) by donning multiple hats, scarves, jumpers and jackets. In fact there's a lot of 'on' going on in Gaelic. In that beautiful tongue you say "the hunger is on me" and "the love that belongs to me is on you." Anger, embarrassment, even names are all said to be "on" a person. I picture the Gaels muffled under layers of feelings and ideas, like our teacher under all her woolly garments.

One evening our Gaelic class was invited to take part in a psychology experiment. University researchers wanted to find out if learning a new language later in life offered any protection against cognitive decay. So they gathered together about forty middle-aged and older learners in a small, hot classroom and asked us to fill in a long questionnaire about our 'language histories'. Most of us were rather tired after a two hour struggle with unfamiliar grammar and vocabulary. Some, like the silvery retired professor who kept asking questions prefaced by "to be clear" were standing on their dignity; others were standing on each other's toes. The atmosphere in the room was quite unpleasant.

The hapless graduate student tasked with establishing the baseline of our cognitive decay was shy and nervous. He played an audio-tape and asked us to count the number of "boings" that we heard. When the boings changed in tone, we were to change the direction of our counting. Now it may be that the student forgot to tell us, or perhaps I missed it but the fact is that I (and I know I wasn't alone in this) did not get the first instruction: "Imagine you are in a lift." So it was very difficult indeed to write down as requested the "final floor number" at the end of each sequence. After a while, someone cottoned on to the lift thing and following a few practice runs we all set to our task. The boings came thick and fast and the changes in tone were rather subtle. After numerous 'boing' sequences, Professor Tobeclear asked "Are we still practising?" I thought the graduate student was going to cry. After what felt like a few more hours of torture, we dutifully handed in our grids filled with numbers. I think the plan was that after a semester of language learning we would be re-tested to see if our boing-counting prowess had deteriorated or improved. But the student never got in contact with us again.

There is a problem with this kind of research. There was so much going on in that room that might have been of interest to a researcher: the impact of tiredness on learning; the phenomenon of irritability; the potential for very clever people to fail to follow simple instructions. I know that my learning of Gaelic has stretched my mind, opened my eyes and nourished my soul. But because we can't measure any of those experiences we count boings instead.

I have no apples at all

After the evening class I moved on to learning Gaelic online, conscientiously repeating phrases and answering quizzes. Then came the superb surprise when I was reading and listening to the lyrics of Grigal Criodhe, or Beloved Gregor. Written as a lament by Gregor's young widow, Marion, it dates back to the 16th century and is achingly sad and beautiful. I came across this sentence:

'Chan eil ubhlan idir agam'

'I have no apples at all'

She regrets that everyone else has apples, but her own, fragrant and spicy like cinnamon, lie low on the ground. It could easily have come from one of my exercises; in fact I am sure I remember repeating it, to learn a grammatical point. But here, towards the end of a beautiful old song, that sentence carries not only all of Marion's grief for her dead husband, but also her memories of sensuous pleasure before he was lost to her.

It was my first real bite of Gaelic.

It seems this is mysterious

Wilson McLeod, Professor of Celtic and Scottish Studies at the University of Edinburgh suggested that I read the opening of 'Hallaig' an iconic poem by Sorley MacLean, one of the foremost Gaelic poets of modern times.

Maclean takes us to the village where his family came from: Hallaig, on the island of Raasay. In a dreamlike atmosphere he conjures up a sadly beautiful place, emptied during the Highland Clearances, and filled now with the dead people who once lived there, glimpsed in the form of native trees.

Entering the wood of Hallaig, I find myself in a time and a place where something has happened that I cannot fully grasp. For an English-speaking reader of Gaelic, so much gets in the way of understanding: not only lack of vocabulary, grammar and cultural context but also my painful awareness of the history of the two languages.

There are patterns and details that Wilson can point out to me. The alternating long and short vowels echo the long and short notes of bagpipe music; the 'West' referred to in the second line is a mythological place away from normal reality, suggesting the past and all the richness of tradition. Wilson also draws my attention to the many times that a particular construction is used. "In Gaelic we have this usage of the preposition "in." We say "I'm in my standing."[tha mi nam sheasamh] or "I'm in my sleep."[tha mi nam chadal.] Ten times it is repeated through this poem. Ten times. It is a part of the shape-shifting, trance-like atmosphere of the poem. This sense of "being in a state of" is completely lost in the English translation."

But there are things that even Wilson doesn't know. I am secretly delighted when he answers my query about the pine cocks in line 13: "It seems this is mysterious." He dismisses my wild guess that they might be capercaillie, but admits that no-one seems to know exactly what they are. The pines certainly are not native to Raasay, and so perhaps the birds are not either, but have come to replace the native species in the way that economic pines supplanted the beautiful broadleaves: rowan, birch and hazel. Once again I am painfully aware of my status as interloper. Like the unlovely, croaking pine-cocks and the pines they inhabit, I am not a graceful native of this place. But being an outsider, an Outlander even, makes it easier for me to raise such questions. I am grateful that he has researched this one for me. I have done my own research, on Google, but on typing in "pine cock" came up only with excitable chatter about an actor's penis appearing on-screen in the Rob Roy film "The Outlaw King." Is this forever now part of the poem for me?

It is while consulting "BBC bite-size" an informative site for school pupils that I find this footnote to Hallaig:

"Cnoc is pronounced 'croc' adding to the effectiveness of the phrase - onomatopoeia reflects the call of the pine cocks (crows)."

With the confidence that can only come from long experience of helping young people to pass their exams, the authors seem to think that they have pinned down those mysterious pine cocks.

Who has the right to interpret a poem? Is appropriation ever a good thing?

A film on my heart

One of the rules that I made for this book was that each poem
or extract was to be no longer than sixteen lines. It was an
arbitrary number, but I wanted to work with pieces that were
short enough to be manageable, that I could pick up and carry
around with me without feeling overwhelmed. Of course, I was
aware of the problems associated with cutting off a poem in
this way, but I decided that I needed to do it.

With Hallaig, it proved impossible to stay within my self-
imposed boundary. I read and re-read the short extract
suggested by Wilson. I waited, as usual, for a line, a word, or
a phrase to strike me, or for an echo from another poem to
come to me, as they usually do. Certainly, the final line of the
extract stayed with me: "chan iadsan coille mo graidh/they are
not the wood I love." I woke up one morning reciting it in
English, and the Gaelic form also resonated. But it was a word
later in the poem that kept coming back to me: 'sgleo.'
MacLean is talking of the ghostly girls of Hallaig, when he
says " 's am boidche 'na sgleo air mo chridhe/and their beauty
a film on my heart." I kept wondering about this phrase. I
imagined a wet, red heart with a membrane across it. How
could the girls' beauty be a film on his heart? Was it
something that got in the way, making it harder to see, or was
it something that added lustre? Or even a cinematic
projection? Seamus Heaney, in his limpid translation, says
"and their beauty a glaze on my heart." Presumably a glaze
protects and enhances. MacBain's Dictionary states that
"sgeol" was used in Gaelic and Irish Bibles to translate Acts
9.18 "Scales fell from his eyes."

This reference recalls for me Dickens' comic description (in
Dombey and Son) of Mrs. Chick's sudden realisation of her
friend Lucretia's treachery:

"Lucretia Tox, my eyes are opened to you all at once. The scales" here Mrs Chick cast down an imaginary pair, such as are commonly used in grocers' shops: "have fallen from my sight."

Grocers' scales being no more familiar to modern readers than opthalmic scales were to poor Mrs. Chick, I take this as a reminder of the likelihood that at least some of my interpretations of MacLean's poem are likely to be wildly and possibly hilariously, inaccurate.

Chapter 4, in which a Poem is forgotten and remembered and other Forgettings are recalled.

Canción de guía by Conrado Nalé Roxlo can be found here: http://poemasdevidayesperanza.blogspot.com/2013/01/cancion-de-guia-1926.html

The Guidebook Song

You have to go through the world as if it didn't matter.

Without asking the name of this bird or that plant,

without asking the Captain of the boat where the water is going.

Look in the opposite direction from where everyone is pointing,

Because it's there that the unexpected rose grows.

Speak with the blacksmith about the horse and the forge,

But all the while looking at the fire, paying careful attention.

Perhaps in a moment of silence you will see the salamander.

Invent a beautiful name for an imaginary woman

And then ask everyone, urgently,

If they have seen her in case they can take you to her house.

Drink hopefully from the empty goblet,

Perhaps a divine madness is held in the glass.

Always take out of your eyes the blue air of your soul,

To see what can never be seen…

English translation by Daphne Loads

I began studying Spanish when I was 15 and ever since I have loved this language with its generous rhythms and painless spelling. The year I left University I went travelling by rail around Spain ending up in Vigo in Galicia, where I taught English as a foreign language.

I sometimes had the feeling we were living in one of those old novels about Brits living in Spain, where the locals are endearingly strange, and hilarious misunderstandings are always happening.

Most evenings I would go to the Street of Wines with two of my fellow teachers. We were known as Las Tres Inglesas (The three English Girls). Our favourite bar was O Porco (The Pig) where we drank opaque red wine out of 'tazas' that looked like miniature toilet bowls and we ate big chunks of tortilla, while the hams hanging round our heads were slowly smoked by the fumes from a hundred Celtas cigarettes. Our nickname for one of the waiters was the Boxer, because of his battered nose. He was remarkably uncommunicative, and we often waited a long time to be served. One week-end my family was visiting from England, so I didn't join my two friends for the evening promenade. The Boxer invited them out for a drink and was relaxed and friendly. He explained that some years before, "tres inglesas" had been friendly with the waiter and his pals. One night they had all gone out together and were involved in a car crash, hence the Boxer's ruined nose. Superstition had reared its ugly head when we arrived, and the boxer and his friend shunned the three of us for fear that history might repeat itself.

Partly to get the Boxer's attention, I had learned to bang my hand down on the counter and say "Da me un vino" so that I got served before anyone noticed that I was a woman, and a foreigner. On one occasion, I was visiting the countryside with my flatmates, Liz and Anton, when we came upon a rough looking but clean little bar. I banged my fist on the wooden counter and demanded drinks. It wasn't until we were leaving, and attempted to pay that we realised we had wandered into someone's kitchen.

Liz was an attractive woman, with dark Spanish looks, although she hailed from Lincolnshire. Many of her students fell in love with her. They could be surprisingly insistent, particularly when they learned that her partner Anton was a vegetarian, and therefore, of course, unable to satisfy her properly. One evening, just before the spring break, one of her moodier students cornered her alone in the classroom and after much sighing and hesitation blurted out, "Miss Liz, I desire you..I desire you...I desire you...!" There was a long pause while Liz looked around her anxiously "… I desire you a happy Easter."

You need someone else to keep comprehending

Felipe Sanchez Burgos is a university lecturer in Santiago, Chile. He uses poetry and other creative methods to teach his students about university teaching. I first met Felipe at an on-line conference, when I immediately warmed to his expressiveness and imagination. Whereas Wilson had selected for me a poem that represented something important in Gaelic literature, Felipe's choice was more personal:

"I tend to recommend things that are difficult to grasp for me. When you share something with another person, there's something about it that's not complete. You need someone else to keep comprehending."

I had often thought of the writing and reading of poems in this way: the reader carrying on the work that has been started by the poet. It had never occurred to me to consider the recommendation of a poem by one reader to another as a similar process. Felipe suggested this particular poem because he had a hunch that it would appeal to me. He also had faith in me that I would be able to engage with what he was offering, both the meanings he understood and those that for him were still missing.

As it happens, the whole poem went missing for a while. Felipe had jumped at the opportunity to choose a poem for me. Having considered and rejected classic Spanish poems of love and sadness, he settled on a piece that he had read recently. But there was a problem. All he had in his mind was the general feeling of the poem: he could recall neither the title nor where he had found it. This is familiar to me: the experience of having a feeling of a poem without the poem itself. There is a very old piece of verse that I came across during my undergraduate years. I have searched but never managed to find it again. What I remember is the image of 'blisse' (bliss) falling like blossom from a tree, and the feeling I have is of the weight of the blossoms, white and scented. As I write I am between hope and fear that someone will get in touch and point me to the exact quotation; then I will have found the missing bliss, but I wonder if that perfect blossom will have been spoiled.

Missing words have always had a fascination for me. When I was seventeen I was called, rather surprisingly to an interview at Girton College, Cambridge. On that frosty December day, I stepped timidly into a book-lined room with a roaring fire where a slender woman with a cigarette in a long holder introduced herself as Lady Radzinowicz. This was my big chance. "Now Daphne", she said, pulling my name into a delightful transatlantic shape. "Tell me about Milton's use of the demotic." I had to admit that I didn't know what demotic meant. She explained and waited patiently for my response. It was then that I admitted to never having read any Milton. One of the world's foremost Milton scholars (as I later found out) threw back her head and laughed. Before the interview I had taken the Common Entrance exam that was then a requirement for application to Cambridge. Lady Radzinowicz waved her cigarette holder at my script. "I'm sorry, she said, but we seem to have lost some pages." The truth was that I had simply stopped, in the middle of a sentence, because I had nothing more to say. I used to wonder if it was the words she imagined to have been written on those mythical missing pages that gave me entrance to the university. I think I've been searching for them ever since.

Eventually Felipe tracked down the missing poem: Canción de Guía by the Argentinian writer and humourist, Conrado Nalé Roxlo. I had assumed that reading the Spanish piece would be more straightforward than peering in to Hallaig. I imagined coming out of the swirling mists of Gaelic into the sunshine of Spanish. Spanish for me has always been a clear, bright language. But this is a paradoxical poem. As Felipe pointed out to me, the guidance begins fairly reasonably, and becomes more and more absurd, until the final completely impossible instruction to see what can never be seen. I notice that the list begins with the certainty of "hay que" (you have to…) but then wanders into some strange contradictions. We are instructed to look away from where people are pointing; that makes me wonder should I look away from where the voice in the poem is pointing? When he tells us to look for the unexpected rose, I find myself, ironically, full of expectation.

In some ways, Felipe is clear what the poem means for him:

"The true meaning behind this is.. you have to push people beyond what they know and see where that takes you. You know that you don't know what you're looking for, but maybe they do. By trying to put the quest for beauty in others, you're open to that beauty because you don't know what it is."

And he points out that that is exactly how he sees the process of construction of this book.

Chapter 5, in which Maria takes liberty with language

A Andorinha da Primavera by Pedro Aires Ferreira de Almeida Gonçalves Magalhães and performed by Madredeus can be found here:
https://music.youtube.com/watch?v=L8vnVoCbAMc&list=RDA MVML8vnVoCbAMc

The Swallow of the Spring

Swallow with a black wing where are you going?

You fly so high

Take me to heaven with you, go

So that up there I can say goodbye to my love

O Swallow

Of the Spring

I wish I could also fly

How good it would be

O Swallow

In the Spring

Also to fly

Translator: Maria de Grade Godinho

Taking liberty with language

Maria is a friend who used to live in Scotland, but moved to Melbourne four years ago. She introduced me to a short song in her native Portuguese, A Andorinha da Primavera : The Spring Swallow. I like the way Maria reads the poem, with her lovely, slightly nasal Portuguese accent. She is from the Alentejo and had wanted to find a poem by a woman from her region, but couldn't come up with one that resonated for her. So she gave me instead this short song written by Pedro Aires Ferreira de Almeida Gonçalves Magalhães and made famous in the 1990s by singer Maria Teresa de Almeida Salgueiro, both members of the group MadreDeus.

Maria chose this piece because of its sense of longing, so familiar to the Portuguese soul. Also she loves the spring and the summer; she was born for warmth (not the cold Scottish winters), and adores the idea of flying. If she had a superpower, she says, it would be the power of flight.

She also liked it because it had the right number of lines, and she didn't need to cut up a longer poem. Was that a shallow reason, she laughingly asked?

I ask Maria about ambiguity and contradictions in poetry. She likes them, she says, and then, in a charming twist on a familiar expression, she says what she really loves is the way that 'poetry takes liberty with language.'

Is Maria's phrase "taking liberty with language" mistaken or inspired?

Chapter 6, in which it proves impossible to make Sense of one old Greek poem, but a Way is found into Another.

I first visited Greece as an inter-railing student in September 1977. On a hillside in Lecithi, Crete, (recalled every time I see the ingredient lecithin listed on a food label) I experienced an intense joy and declared that I wanted to stay there forever. I promptly and accidentally dropped my spectacles down the hillside and didn't wear specs again for many years. I went back, 40 years later, but I didn't find the specs. Or that feeling.

Erotokritos

by Vikentios Kornaros

1	Κι ωσάν από μικρόν αυγό πουλί μικρόν εβγαίνει,
2	Τρεμουλιασμένο κι άφαντο και με καιρό πληθαίνει,
3	Κάνει κορμί, κάνει φτερά, καθ' ώρα μεγαλώνει
4	Και πορπατεί, χαμοπετά, φτερούγια του ξαπλώνει,
5	Κι απ' άφαντο κι από μικρό πού 'τον, όντεν εφάνη,
6	Κορμί, φτερά και δύναμη και μεγαλότη κάνει,
7	Το ίδιο εγίνει κ' εις εμέ, στην άπραγή μου νιότη:
8	Αρχή μικρή κι αψήφιστη έτον από την πρώτη,
9	μά εδά 'χει τόση δύναμη κ' έτσι μεγάλη εγίνη,
10	όπου μου πήρε την εξά και δίχως νου μ' αφήνει.

11   Κ' η αγάπη, πού στα βάσανα αντρεύγει και πληθαίνει

12   Και με τους αναστεναγμούς θρέφεται και χορταίνει,

13   Θάμασμα πούρι το κρατούν όλοι, μικροί μεγάλοι,

14   Πώς στην αρχή τση ανήμπορη γεννάται, στην αθάλη:

15   Σπίθα μικρή και αψήφιστη, δε λάμπει μηδέ βράζει

16   Και πως να κάνει αναλαμπή κιανείς δε το λογιάζει·

Erotokritos

1   Just like a bird, emerging new-born from the egg,

2   Little and frail, but then in time it thrives,

3   Builds up its body and plume, growing by the hour,

4   And walks, stretching its wings and tries them out and flies,

5   From weak and little that it was at first when it emerged,

6   Now it has body and wings and strength,

7   Such a thing happened to me, to my naive youth:

8   It started small, easy to ignore - initially it was

9   But it has so much power now, so vast it turned out

10   It took away my peace of mind, and left me without.

11   Love, when troubled, becomes braver and stronger,

12   Feeding on the desperate sighs,

13   It is indeed a wonder, anyone, young and old can tell,

14   How from the ashes it is born, feeble at first,

15   Only a spark, you would ignore, without glow nor flame,

16   No one believes the blaze that spark became.

English translation by Smaragda Tsaridou

Smaragda trained as an opera singer in her native Greece, and now writes and sings folk and contemporary music. She also works as an educator at the University of Edinburgh, which is where I met her over a decade ago. Smaragda suggested to me a short extract from the 17th century poem, Erotokritos, in the Sitian dialect of Crete.

How can I get anywhere with this poem? I have Smaragda's assurance that it has elegance in Greek. She loves the way it describes the beginnings of love, growing slowly until it becomes impossible to ignore. For her it represents a way back from understanding poetry as merely something to be passed in an exam. I also have her lovely reading and her own translation. And yet, I fail to find a way in.

I am meeting Smaragda for coffee in Edinburgh. She tells me about her new job. She asks me how the book is going, and I tell her the familiar tale of rejection and persistence. Oh by the way, I say, the other Greek poem, by coincidence, it's a poem from Crete! There is a fleeting look in her dark eyes, a look of what, exactly? Confusion? Disappointment? but our conversation moves on, and I don't register that look until I'm on the bus home, and I realise I've muddled the two Greek poems in my head. Konstantina's poem is associated with her home town in mainland Greece. Throughout the making of this book, I have found mistakes to be fruitful, chance encounters with my subconscious to show that it is going on working underneath everything else. But this seems to be a mis-step that only throws into question my trustworthiness. My bold insistence that I have a right to explore poems in other languages, despite, and even because of my mistakes melts away. But the conversation has moved on. Smaragda tells me that there is something she wanted to ask me - she is planning to record a sung version of Erotokritos, and asks my permission to use the translation of the extract she has given me. Her carefulness contrasts with my carelessness.

To γεφύρι της Άρτας (extract)

Ως τρέμει το καρυόφυλλο, να τρέμει το γιοφύρι,

κι ως πέφτουν τα δεντρόφυλλα, να πέφτουν οι διαβάτες."

"Κόρη, τον λόγον άλλαξε κι άλλη κατάρα δώσε,

πο 'χεις μονάκριβο αδελφό, μη λάχει και περάσει."

Κι αυτή το λόγον άλλαζε κι άλλη κατάρα δίνει:

"Αν τρέμουν τ' άγρια βουνά, να τρέμει το γιοφύρι,

κι αν πέφτουν τ' άγρια πουλιά, να πέφτουν οι διαβάτες,

τί έχω αδελφό στην ξενιτιά, μη λάχει και περάσει.

"…May the bridge ever shake, as carnations shake,

And may those who cross it ever fall down, as leaves fall from trees."

"Girl, take that back, make it a different curse,

Because you have your only dear brother, lest he happen to pass by."

And so she took it back and uttered a different curse:

"When the wild mountains shake, then may the bridge shake,

And when the wild birds fall from the sky, then may those who cross it fall.

For I have a brother abroad, lest he happen to pass by."

English Translation by Michael Tziotis

I can see them falling

Konstantina was adamant: the song that she had chosen did not contain any hidden meanings. She knew that songs and poems can reveal something of our inner worlds, but not this one. She had learned it at school, with all the other children because it was about their bridge in their town. The song was very famous throughout Greece. It referred to the ancient practice of human sacrifice, and it could be interpreted as a fable about the conflict between personal feeling and community duty. But there was nothing else to say, particularly for someone like her who, she claimed, knew nothing of poetry.

It is an old story that tells of the building of the Bridge of Arta that can still be seen today, spanning the calm waters of the Aracthos river in Western Greece. In ancient times the river was wild and prone to flooding, and the local people needed a bridge to be able to cross it safely. But despite the best efforts of the bridge builders, the Aracthos could not be spanned.

Every day they worked hard to build a bridge, only to find that during the night it had been reduced to rubble. Eventually a mysterious, speaking bird told them what was needed: a human sacrifice. Not just anyone would do: it had to be the beautiful young wife of the master builder. Reluctantly he called for her and when she came she was tricked into going down into a chamber of the bridge. Realising that she was to be sacrificed, she brought down a terrible curse: whoever crossed the bridge would fall to their death. People remonstrated with her, saying what if her beloved brother were to cross the bridge, so she relented and changed her curse to a blessing.

I was sure that there was something there, just out of reach. When I listened to Konstantina's recording I heard her beautiful voice rising and falling. I could feel the rhythm of the song; I just couldn't find my way in to it. We had been talking for a while, a little haltingly, as if my earnest questioning about ambiguity and contradiction was unwelcome and rather missed the point. But then I asked Konstantina if any word or phrase particularly resonated for her, and she said "Yes. When the people fall, like leaves, I can see them falling. And I like the way the curse is changed – just a tiny change to the words that make it into a blessing." She had shown me a way into the song.

What does it mean, to get into a poem? Is it like getting into a warm pair of pyjamas and a comfy bed? Sometimes it feels a bit like getting into a situation you're unsure of: what are we getting into here? Sometimes it's like getting into line, or getting into trouble. And often the poem gets into me. I remember as a school girl reading a sexy book and discussing it on the bus with my friend. I loved the part where it said "before sunset they were inside each other." Don't be stupid, said my friend, it says "he was inside her." Funny how our innocent mistakes hint at possibilities we cannot yet imagine.

Are you able to get into this Greek poem? Why/why not?

Chapter 7 In which the Author meets three excellent Gentlemen and experiences the Mozart effect

O Doctorze Hiszpanie

Jan Kochanowski

"Nasz dobry doktor spać się od nas bierze,

Ani chce z nami doczekać wieczerze".

"Dajcie mu pokój! najdziem go w pościeli,

A sami przedsię bywajmy weseli!"

"Już po wieczerzy, pódźmy do Hiszpana!"

"Ba, wierę, pódźmy, ale nie bez dzbana".

"Puszczaj, doktorze, towarzyszu miły!"

Doktor nie puścił, ale drzwi puściły.

"Jedna nie wadzi, daj ci Boże zdrowie!"

"By jeno jedna" - doktor na to powie.

Od jednej przyszło aż więc do dziewiąci,

A doktorowi mózg się we łbie mąci.

"Trudny - powiada - mój rząd z tymi pany:

Szedłem spać trzeźwo, a wstanę pijany".

"Our doctor intends to leave us and go to sleep.

He doesn't even want to wait until the end of the dinner.

Let him in peace, we will find him in bed.

And meanwhile, let us be merry.

The dinner is finished; let's go to the Spaniard.

Let's go, yes, but not without the ewer.

Let us in our Doctor, our kind host!

Doctor didn't let us in. But the doors did.

One glass won't hurt, God may give you good health.

But only one glass, the doctor replies.

From one it went up to nine,

and doctor's brain is turning in his head.

Something is wrong in me in the company of these gentlemen.

I went to sleep sober, but I will wake up drunk.

English translation: Tomas Bak

I have very little knowledge of Polish. At first sight a Scrabble-player's dream with its pile-ups of consonants, and favouring of x, y j and z, it sounds like a chewy, meaty language. I have been told it is a good language for expressing emotions, and that the months have charming names: February means 'fierce' and the word for April is 'flowery.' That's all I know.

In sixteenth century Poland, a group of men are enjoying dinner and a few drinks. Amongst them is Jan Kochanowski, the poet credited with giving Poles a literary language of their own and who left us such moving poetry about the death of his little girl, Urszula. Having grown up quietly in rural Poland, Jan travelled and studied in Italy, France and Germany before coming to the court of King Sigismund II in Krakow. Eventually he will tire of the court and its intrigues and retire to the Black Forest to write poetry, but this evening he is in good spirits. Among the dinner guests is his friend and fellow scholar and courtier, Pedro Ruiz de Moros, a native of Aragona, who has also travelled widely. Well-integrated in the local culture, he nevertheless has been known to rebuke his Polish friends for their "overdrinking." He is the Spanish Doctor immortalised in this short poem by Kochanowski and included in "Fraszki", his volume of light-hearted but deep "Trifles". Long before the others have finished eating and drinking, de Moros is ready for his bed and soberly takes his leave. Unabashed, his friends continue merrymaking and eventually follow him uninvited into his bedroom where, against his mild protests they get the sleepy doctor to down nine glasses of wine. The Doctor notes that something strange is happening: "I went to sleep sober, but I will wake up drunk!"

The Mozart Effect

The 21st century guide who has introduced me to these characters is another well-travelled and well-educated man, Thomas Bak. Thomas reads the poem for me in his native Polish, with a warm, rich accent moving lightly between the different voices, so that I hear the humour and feel the warmth. He says it's such a pleasure to recite this: Kochanowski's 500 year-old poem is completely intelligible to a modern Polish ear. "It's like he could be in the next room from you." One line has become a familiar contemporary expression in Polish, because it is so funny. " 'The doctor didn't let us in…but the doors did.' An elegant way of saying they broke in!" In fact, Thomas has often thought that he would like to have dinner with this erudite man, well-versed in classical and modern languages, who loved life, could laugh at himself and was very good company. For Thomas, this is humanism, not just an intellectual movement, but a certain very human attitude to life.

Only 14 lines long, the poem uses plain words and doesn't waste a syllable. Thomas admires this economy and simplicity: "Poetry tries to shed the irrelevant things, concentrating on the crucial bits." (How different from Sophia's views on irrelevance in Chapter 8).My challenge for Thomas is to help me understand the beauty that he sees in this poem. He likes the German word for poetry, [Dichtung]which comes from [dicht]meaning dense. "There are two things here: one is the density and the second is the light simplicity. I would call it almost a Mozart effect."

As Thomas speaks of light simplicity and density together, I am reminded of a favourite piece of mine, by another courtier-poet and also from the 16th century: Sir Thomas Wyatt's "They flee from me that sometime did me seek." The two poems make an interesting pair. Certainly the light simplicity and condensed meanings are there in both pieces, and the same startling readability across the centuries. But Kochanowski is in a humorous, tolerant state of mind, and Wyatt's mood is bitter. While the characters in the Polish poem are funny and likeable, those in the English poem are as unpredictable and unknowable as wild creatures. Whereas De Moros has merely been manoeuvred into having a few extra glasses of wine, the narrator of Wyatt's poem seems to have been cruelly betrayed.

Chapter 8 In which Mum despairs and Sofia introduces Slut Poetry

You can find the poem, 《你没有看见我被遮蔽的部分》 here: https://poemwiki.org/p/MTYwOTY5Njk2OTY3NzQ=

You didn't see my covered part by Yu Xihua

In spring, I cite flowers, flames, canopies on the cliff

But there is still a lonely cry in the rain, which beats the clouds like a blunt weapon

It's always too late to love, and it's already deep. I bite your name and bleed

But did not open the gloomy seal

Those light parts let me stop: canna, black butterfly, reflection in the water

I said: hello, hello. Please accept my bowing love

But I have never been deceived, never

Like a river, in the deepest night, I know where tomorrow is going

But in the end I still can't forgive myself for keeping you so complete

You still don't know those illusions

How much dust is needed in the world to cover a woman

Bloody but still glowing affection

English translation: Google Translate

When Winter comes

Mum was not what you'd call a carefree person. At six months old she was badly burned when her wooden cot caught fire. Her hair never grew in properly and ever after she had angry scarring on her face. Her toddler sister who raised the alarm by shouting: "Burn! Burn!" grew up to be a beauty with thick, wavy, dark locks. After that, Mum experienced her life as a series of losses. All of her teeth were taken out at once by a dentist in a hurry; she bled copiously with difficult periods every month; her biggest loss, my arrival, came when my sisters were grown up and she felt she was past the age of childbearing. Mum expressed her huge unhappiness with a small repertoire of gloomy sayings that she repeated over and over again. I later discovered that one of these was the last line of "Ode to the West Wind." In Shelley's poem there is a question mark, and the answer he seems to expect is an encouraging "no."

"If Winter comes, can Spring be far behind?"

Based on her own experiences of long, cold times, for Mum the answer was a resounding "yes!" She also changed the "if" to the sad certainty of "when."

"When Winter comes, can Spring be far behind!"

Some would say that my mother's particular unhappiness is irrelevant to Shelley's universal ode: poets work with what we all share, not what individuals bring with them; and yet Mum's pain is forever a part of Shelley's poem for me. Somehow she managed to turn one of the most hopeful lines in all of English Literature into a cry of despair.

There is a line in Milton's Paradise Lost that goes:"Flowers of all Hue and without Thorn the Rose."I am struck by the momentary pause between with and out, the contrast between presence and absence. With..out With…out Now you have it, now you don't. I have always liked to read so closely that I seem to slip in between the words, and even between the two halves of a word. With ..out…with…out. Like the old joke about the car indicator light. "Is it working?" "Yes. No. Yes. No."

Sans, senza, sin, sem, meneria. I learned the word "without" in the language of every country I visited, because I hate raw onions with a vengeance, and need to be able to say "without onions." The word reminds me so much of Mum. For her it was as if Shakespeare's seventh age of man had come early: and she found herself "Sans teeth, sans eyes, sans taste, sans everything." It was in the first age that she began to lose everything – first her hair before it had even grown in, then her teeth and, repeatedly, her blood.

Speaking Chinese with some of the letters missed out

There's a great line in the Suzy Bogguss song about miscommunication between the sexes: "She said, he heard." It comes in the middle of an argument when the woman suddenly realises that her male partner doesn't understand a word she's saying. "He looked at me like I was speaking Chinese…with some of the letters missed out." For English speakers, Chinese is often a lazy byword for the incomprehensible, but here the masterstroke is to add "with some of the letters missed out." How would he know? And in any case, Chinese doesn't have letters, does it? Our ignorance of the most widely spoken language in the world is alarming, and our lack of awareness of the extent of that ignorance is absurd. Personally I know only how to say "Nee hao."

Some sort of reflection of myself

Sofia is a Mandarin-speaking ex-colleague who chose for me a poem by the contemporary Chinese poet, Yu Xihua, 《你没有看见我被遮蔽的部分》 ("You didn't see my covered part"). Yu Xihua overcame many barriers as a disabled, poor, woman from a rural area to become famous in China for what is known as 'slut poetry.' Sofia tells me that this is because her writing is so "wild and free" and deals very openly with feelings, including sexual feelings. When I asked if the title referred to the woman's genitals, she said, "no, probably not," and I felt a bit silly.

At the time when she chose the piece, Sofia had just been through a painful breakup. Before, she had clung to an absolute belief in love and the idea that if you love someone you must do everything to be with them. Following the painful break with her ex, Sofia said she had begun to find a deeper understanding of "the complexity of humanity, love and commitment." It seems she was able to use the poem as a mirror in which to see her own feelings and experiences. Sofia says, "The last section is some sort of reflection of myself...it is talking about what I felt."

The Beholder's Share

Both my mother and Sofia bring their own meanings to poems, independently of the author's intention or other readers' interpretations. Each of them is taking what is known in art history as "The Beholder's Share." This is the notion that both artist and viewer contribute something to the making of a painting. I love that phrase: "The Beholder's Share." It calls to mind the old adage "Beauty is in the eye of the beholder" and at the same time contradicts it. The onus is not on the beholder, since both the responsibilities and the satisfactions of art are shared. It also has an echo of "The Angel's Share": that part of the whisky that is lost to evaporation during the aging process. Whisky being more commonly associated with the devil, it is delightful to think that angels might also enjoy a wee dram. And finally, that word 'beholder': not 'viewer' or 'audience' or 'critic', but the one who beholds, from Old English [bi] thoroughly and [haldan] to hold. The beholder is someone who holds on tightly to the poem.

At the time when Sophia sent me "You didn't see my covered part," she was very busy, and I didn't want to ask her to translate it, so I put it through Google Translate instead. Sofia said that the resulting English version was really good: "It's basically what it means." But I was surprised to discover how unstable, or perhaps dynamic, the Google translation was. I submitted the Mandarin poem repeatedly, and it came out slightly differently every time. The first time I read the first line:

"In spring, I raised flowers, flames and crowns on cliffs"

I saw a solitary figure semaphoring from the top of a cliff, waving flowering and burning branches, and metallic crowns in some kind of ritual. But the following week 'raised' had become "cited" and this seemed to me a much less flamboyant start. The poet, it seemed was talking about quoting the words of others, in a way that was familiar to both Sofia and I as academics.

The final line also kept changing between versions. The first time it was presented as:

'A flirty but still glowing affection'

But 'flirty' became first 'bloody' and then 'blood-fleshed.' When I asked Sofia she said she understood the word as describing what happens when someone is cut, mixing blood and flesh together. It reminded me of what was happening as I read the different translations: the constituent parts of the poem were being mashed together, and were still very impressive.

The thing that perplexed me most was a word that remained consistent. In every version there are four 'buts,' suggesting oppositions that I cannot fully comprehend. (Once again I am troubled by "but."See Chapter 9).

I was struck by Sofia's comment that what meant most to her were the seemingly irrelevant parts of the poem – "canna, black butterfly, reflection in water." Unlike Thomas, in Chapter 7 who loves Jan Kochanowski's poetry for its lack of any irrelevant matter, Sofia likes what she called "the irrelevant parts" best of all : "canna, black butterfly, reflection in the water." These seemingly random elements she appropriates for her own purposes. She seems to use Yu Xihua's poem as a frame on which to stretch out her own feelings and experiences. Strangely what seems least relevant to Sophia, means the most to her. Relevance is a fascinating concept. When I was a university teacher, we were often urged to make our disciplines more 'relevant' to students and their lives. This was usually taken to mean making connections with TV shows, current affairs or internet memes. But I found that relevance was something that students had to make for themselves. As with our understanding of "the Beholder's Share" etymology may again be helpful here. By studying how a particular word has derived from earlier forms, and how it has been used at different times and in different contexts, we can learn a lot about what it means for us. Relevant comes from the Latin [relevare] to raise up. So something that is relevant is something that is raised up where we can see it. I don't think it pops up automatically, like a tripped switch. It's more that we are all responsible for the raising. The poet who flags up the significance of the word; the beholder who holds it up to their own light, and each of us who uses the word over and over again, leaving behind our marks and echoes for future generations.

Daphne's Scisssors

I love to collect snowdrops. I recently came across a variety called "Daphne's Scissors" for the tiny scissor-shaped green markings on its white petals. Something about the idea of my personalised pair of scissors caught my attention. It seems to me that relevance is less about the inherent qualities that any word or object has, but rather that everything is relevant to everything else and what we each have is a pair of scissors with which to cut out particular parts as we see fit.

What can machines tell us about poetry?

Chapter 9 In which the Author handles Hassle badly and ponders the Expression of Love.

The Book of Love, by Nizar Kabbani can be found here:
https://www.noor-book.com/en/ebook

I hate to love like other people

I hate to write like other people

I wish my mouth was a church

And my letters were bells…

Love, my dear

Is a beautiful poem written on the moon

Love is drawn on all the foliage

Love is engraved on the feathers of birds

And rain drops

But any woman in my country

Who loves a man

Gets stoned with fifty stones

English translation: Mourad Diouri

When I first arrived in Cairo as a young woman in 1984, I was overwhelmed by the attention I received. Men followed me on the street and made lewd or fatuous comments. For the first time in my life I disengaged the part of my brain that is interested in foreign languages. I simply did not want to know what they were saying to me.

It was more than 30 years before I studied Arabic again. I had been told of a very good teacher called "Philomena"who gave classes at the university where I worked. I imagined a pleasant, middle-aged Irishwoman. It turned out that Phil Hermena was an Armenian man who, with patience and good humour helped me to make peace with the beautiful Arabic language.

لكن – lakin - but

My ex-colleague Mourad was my guide for the Arabic chapter. He chose an extract from The Book of Love by the Syrian poet Nizar Kabbani, one of his favourite pieces to use in teaching Arabic at the University of Edinburgh. He explained that even beginning students can understand it because of the simplicity of Kabbani's words and that this brings them into direct contact with authentic literature. When Mourad read the poem to me, I could only pick out a few words that I recognised.

Lakin (but) was one of them. Why did that word jump out at me? I think it took me back to when I was in Egypt. At that time and in that place, I couldn't manage to reconcile so many contradictions. Religious men had dark bruises where they banged their heads on the ground to pray, but those same men muttered obscenities to me as I passed. My friend Rosemary knew me as a respectful and gentle person, but she saw me spit in the street at a man who insulted her: she wanted to get me out of there on the next plane home. My friend Hoda had been married for twenty-five years, and loved her husband deeply, but she could never admit that she had fallen in love with him before they were introduced, for fear of seeming "easy."

In explaining his choice of poem, Mourad said:

"The topic of love, it's universal, a positive subject for everyone. Noone would object to hearing that. It is a beautiful thing."

But I thought of Hoda.

Have you ever fallen out of love with a language?

Chapter 10 In which the Author says farewell to the Poet's Wife.

Musumbavhaloi

F E Mutshaeni

Ranga nga yau say a tshiivha u sumba.

Musumbavaloi, zwau elelwa u ranga, u sumbe

Ranga nga lau dandu u bvisa.

Ngalo vhanwe tshenzhemo I dale

Munwe u disumba, u gude.

Musumbavhaloimutata u sumbwa

Mushaya tshimubelwa kha lothea tshi kala

Na mufuwi a siho wa lothe

Musumbavhaloi guda u gudese

U gudese u khagala lwa phatho u sumba

Maitele na mbuya tsumbo khagala nga iwe

Zwinw nga mbilu u itelwa wa emula

Kha vhothe u itela simesa.

U sumbe lwa phatho na ndaedzo u tonde.

Forefinger

Start by pointing at your own chest

Think of your own mistakes and direct the forefinger at your own beam first before pointing at another person's speck

So as to provide onlookers with valuable experience

Learn to point at yourself first.

The forefinger : one who dislikes being pointed at.

While there is no one without any wrongdoing that warrants him to be pointed at.

However, you should learn to openly point positively.

Openly point for good and constructive reasons.

Whatever you wish others to do for you.

Do it generously for others too.

Always point constructively to others and for direction-giving with a warm attitude.

English translation by Nancy Mutshaeni and F.E. Mutshaeni

Tshivenda is one of 10 official languages of South Africa, spoken by 1.2 million people in Limpopo Province. Professor Humbulani Nancy Mutshaeni introduced me to this sonnet, which was written by her husband, F.E. Mutshaeni. Nancy was Director of the Centre for Higher Education at the University of Venda.

We did not get the chance to discuss her chosen poem. Nancy had a high profile role in her University and was very busy. When we did find a time that we could both meet, connection problems got in the way. Most frustrating of all was 'load shedding' which happens when power companies temporarily switch off the electricity supply to protect South Africa's overloaded system. "So many obstacles" as Nancy said. A few months after our last email exchange, I was checking Nancy's official job title online, when I came across her obituary. Now any questions I have for her will never be answered.

Metaphors

I spot the neat green star-shaped shoots in March. By April I'm on my knees, fighting the annual battle against bluebells. Beautiful as they are, they could easily take over the whole garden, sucking up air and moisture, and leaving less robust specimens to die. I seldom dig deep enough to root out the translucent white bulbs, so they generally come back stronger the following year. Sometimes an unpleasant zeal overtakes me and I find that I have grubbed out miniature daffodils and choice white celandines – the very plants I hoped to save.

When Dad died, my strange, estranged sister scattered his ashes in a bluebell wood. It was a good choice, but she did it without consultation, and for reasons of her own refused to tell us the location of his last resting place. One April day I was on the phone to a friend, stoking my resentment towards my sister, when I happened to look out into the garden, and saw a familiar splash of blue. "I don't need to go and find Dad's ashes in any particular place." I said, "He'll always be with me, like the bluebells." That was several years ago, shortly after I had planted a small colony of bluebells in my front garden. Colony – there's the clue. Over the years they have gradually taken over, in league with the equally invasive and equally beautiful Alchemilla. Every April, my pious words come back to haunt me. Dad would have laughed.

Metaphors are a bit like bluebells. We start by placing them carefully. Then they place themselves, and eventually replace everything else. The parable in this poem is so familiar – take out the plank of wood from your own eye, before trying to help the person with a speck of sawdust in theirs. It has never occurred to me before, but the Pythonesque quality of the metaphor strikes me now.

Nancy told me that in Tshivendi the index is known as the finger that points out witches. As I write those Scottish women (and some men) who were executed for witchcraft are being pardoned.

Chapter 11 In which the Author enjoys the Slippages between Languages, and stumbles through an Italian Poem.

Chi cade by Chandra Livia Candiani can be found here: https://bodosproject.blogspot.com/2018/02/chi-cade-di-chandra-livia-candiani.html

Those who fall

Glorious mystery

The face of the world

Beneath the weaving of names,

Fair of blood

The wounds come to red

To sew the light.

At the heart of the night

(the night has a heart)

Encircling darkness

Ego is drifting

Someone who does not think of you –

Almost never.

Get in your own shoes

And get to dance.

English translation: Gaia del Negro

Sitting in a leafy Lisbon cafe, I was chatting with my colleague Steve, an English teacher who had recently arrived from Milan. When Steve asked for a coffee, the waiter thanked him for his order and returned with a cup and saucer in one hand and a large sizzling snack in the other. Steve groaned, "Not again!" He had quickly discovered that his polite Italian "prego" actually means "steak sandwich" in Portuguese, but he just couldn't get out of the habit of repeating it every time someone said 'thank you.' I love these delicious slippages between languages.

I learned my Italian from Harold, an old man who lived opposite Girton, in those days an all-women's College where I was studying English. Every Wednesday evening, three or four young undergraduates would go across the road to his house to read Dante. I think he was a retired academic, who liked to pass on his knowledge and wisdom to the next generation. My lack of curiosity about Harold surprises me now, but my lack of suspicion about his motives does not: I was very innocent. We dutifully did our homework, and prepared weekly translations, taking turns to read them out. One day I came across this line from the Purgatorio:

"Or vedi figlio: tra Beatrice e te è questo muro."

My translation was, I think, accurate, but it came out in a comic accent, as if a Yorkshire builder were passing on advice to his young apprentice.

"Now look, son, between Beatrice and you there's this wall."

I understood that the wall in Dante's poem stood for something more than bricks and mortar, and I remember being delighted by the hilarious juxtaposition of the humdrum and the metaphysical.

When I read the poem that Gaia del Negro had chosen for me I missed this easy movement between the day-to-day and the profound. Gaia had selected a piece called Chi Cade, by the Milanese poet Chandra Livia Candini. Gaia tells me that Candini is well-known throughout Milan and the whole of Italy, for her work in translating Buddhist texts and in teaching meditation. In particular she likes to work in poor inner city areas, making poetry with multi-cultural groups of children.

Gaia herself is an independent researcher, an educator, and a teacher of Italian as a foreign language. She teaches through movement and it seemed entirely fitting that she danced her way through the lines, while I found myself galumphing along behind. Gaia loves this poem for its complexity and mystery. I warmed to it a little when Gaia read it out to me, but I struggled to get into it. The problem was not with my lack of knowledge. I am grateful that I am, as Keats put it, "capable of being in uncertainties, mysteries, doubts, without any irritable reaching after fact & reason": I usually love the mysteriousness of poetry. But right from the start this poem made me feel glum. The phrase "glorious mystery" reminds me of Sunday School. The songs they taught us were all about the glory and splendour of God, and yet they were overwhelmingly dreary and dark. And what could I make of that "face of the world"? A human face is the most accessible of things: the tiniest baby can make out a face. But here it feels remote and untouchable: like the North Face of the Eiger, or the faces of a polyhedron in a maths problem at school.

For Gaia, the words for familiar things, weaving, dancing, the night, lead easily to great questions. Who weaves the names? Who names things? How? What happens? How to explore the night with a trusting heart? For her, weaving is a very human gesture, most associated with women. She is interested in the holes in the weaving, in the connections, the fact that 'tessitura' refers to both the action of weaving and the object that is woven. In the act of weaving she says, some things are hidden and some are made known. What is beneath the weaving? But unlike Gaia I found the poem difficult to get hold of; I couldn't find a grammatical thread.

We both liked this line: "At the heart of the night (the night has a heart)"

Gaia pointed out how "nel cuore de la notte" is a very commonplace expression for the middle of the night. The metaphor comes back to life when the poet points out to us that the night has a real heart, as Gaia put it "a bumping heart" and again I felt a dead metaphor come to life.

We also enjoyed the mistakes that we made in each other's languages. I thought that 'vengon' had something to do with vengeance: it simply means "come" and Gaia wrote "to saw" for "to sew."

"Fallen" reminds Gaia that when we dance, we fall. I had never thought of dancing as falling, but suddenly I see it as a continuous, creative response to gravity: every step is a footfall, every leap up returns to fall down. I found so poignant the way that Gaia's otherwise graceful English translation made a clumsy ending. 'Get in your own shoes and get to dance.' It seemed to capture perfectly my fumbling with the words in the poem, while she simply put on her shoes and danced.

Chapter 12 in which the Author reflects on what She has learned

Understanding, misunderstanding, being an outsider, forgetting

So what have I learned from reading these eleven poems chosen for me by my friends? First of all, I have been reminded of how reading poetry can intensify experience, and bring understanding of ourselves and the world. My faith has been confirmed in the preposterous idea that we can receive these benefits even from poems written in foreign languages.

I have known again the hard work and time it takes to get into a poem, and the sad truth that, sometimes however hard I try I will be left outside.

I have also come to appreciate the important role of misunderstanding, what Christopher Ricks calls that "divine dyslexia" that leads us to create new meanings through what we miss, mistake and misinterpret. Foreigners and beginners are especially prone to such creative blunders and I have grown to understand my preference for being the outsider, and the blessings that this can bring.

Finally I have rediscovered the power of forgotten poems, those strange entities that we bump into when we are groping in the dark.

So, what do you make of this book?

Printed in Great Britain
by Amazon